Natural BEAUTY

Compiled by Dan Zadra • Edited by Kristel Wills • Designed by Jessica Phoenix

COMPENDIUM™
incorporated

ACKNOWLEDGEMENTS
These quotations were gathered lovingly but unscientifically over several years and/or were contributed by many friends or acquaintances. Some arrived—and survived in our files—on scraps of paper and may therefore be imperfectly worded or attributed. To the authors, contributors and original sources, our thanks, and where appropriate, our apologies. –The Editors

WITH SPECIAL THANKS TO
Jason Aldrich, Gerry Baird, Jay Baird, Neil Beaton, Josie Bissett, Laura Boro, Jim and Alyssa Darragh & Family, Marta and Kyle Drevniak, Jennifer and Matt Ellison & Family, Rob Estes, Michael and Leianne Flynn & Family, Sarah Forster, Jennifer Hurwitz, Heidi Jones, Carol Anne Kennedy, June Martin, Tom DesLongchamp, Steve and Janet Potter & Family, Diane Roger, Kirsten and Garrett Sessions, Andrea Shirley, Clarie Yam and Erik Lee, Kobi and Heidi Yamada & Family, Justi and Tote Yamada & Family, Bob and Val Yamada, Kaz and Kristin Yamada & Family, Tai and Joy Yamada, Anne Zadra, August and Arline Zadra, and Gus and Rosie Zadra.

CREDITS
Compiled by Dan Zadra
Edited by Kristel Wills
Designed by Jessica Phoenix

ISBN: 978-1-932319-80-4

1st Printing. 20K 10 08

Printed with soy ink in China

Some people add more beauty to the world just by being in it.

Beauty is everywhere and all around us—not just in nature, but in human nature. Most of the beautiful things in life come by twos and threes, by dozens or thousands. Lots of flowers, stars, sunsets, seashells, rainbows, mountains—but only one unique and unrepeatable you in all of nature.

Elizabeth Cady Stanton believed that, when it comes to matters of the heart, nature never repeats herself—that the possibilities of one human soul will never be replicated in another.

And so the thoughts in these pages celebrate what is real, genuine, joyful and unrepeatable in the human spirit. They celebrate the kind of beauty that can never fade. After all, those whom we experience with joy are always beautiful, always appreciated and never forgotten.

When you begin, begin at the beginning. Begin with
magic, begin with the sun, begin with the grass.

Helen Wolfert

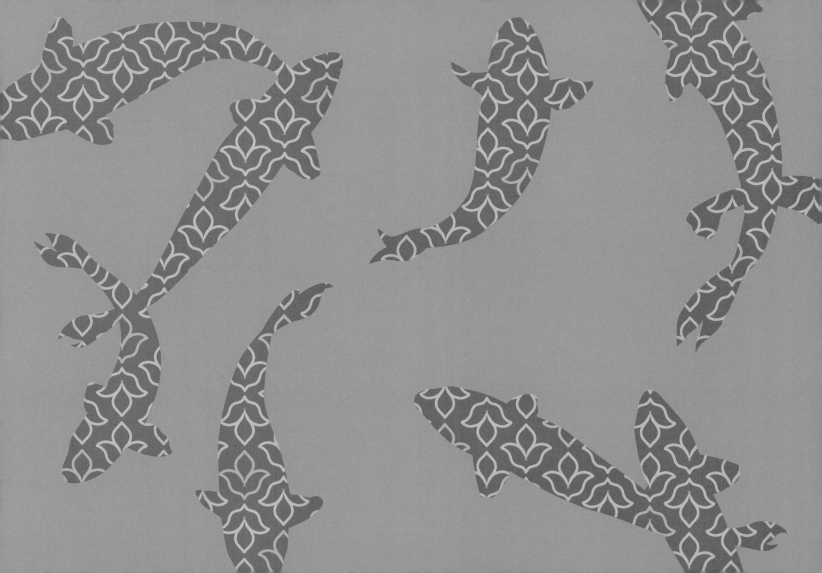

We're here to feel the joy of life pulsing in us now.

Joyce Carol Oates

Joy is where your life began, with your first cry. Joy is your birthright.

Sarah Ban Breathnach

Go out, go out I beg of you. And taste the beauty of the wild. Behold the miracle of the earth. With all the wonder of a child.

Edna Jacques

Sit outside at midnight and close your eyes; feel the grass, the air, the space.

Listen to birds for ten minutes at dawn. Memorize a flower.

Linda Hasselstrom

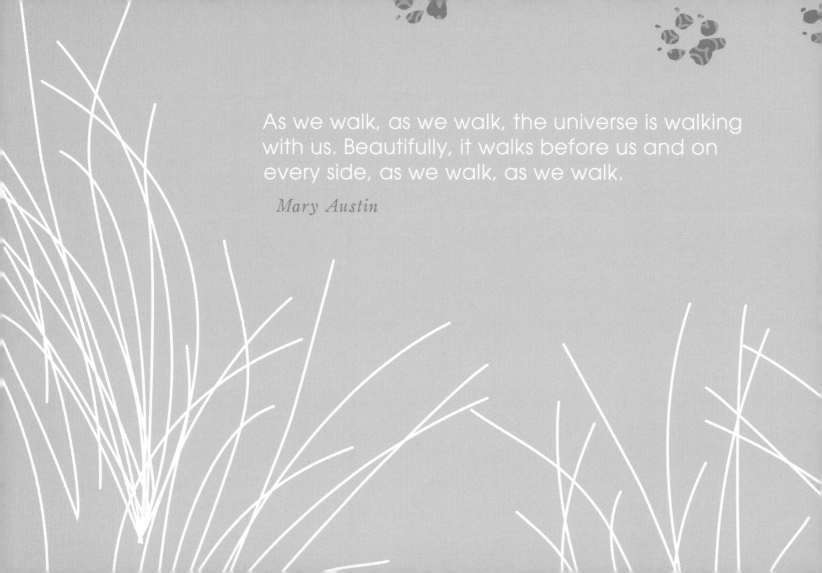

As we walk, as we walk, the universe is walking with us. Beautifully, it walks before us and on every side, as we walk, as we walk.

Mary Austin

And we are nature. We are nature seeing nature.
The red-winged blackbird flies in us....

Susan Griffin

She knew things that nobody had ever told her.
For instance, the words of the trees and the wind.

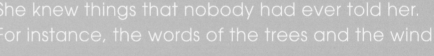

Zora Neale Hurston

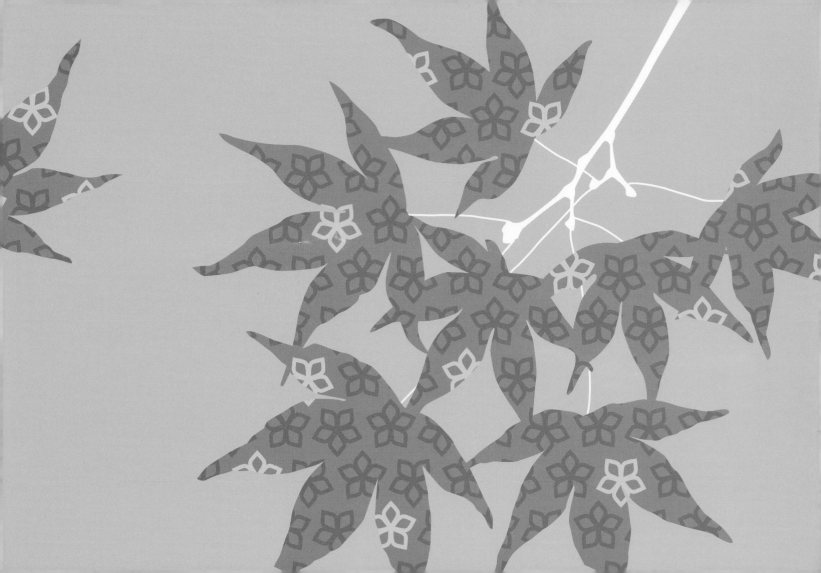

Wind moving through grass so that the grass quivers. This moves me with an emotion that I don't even understand.

Katherine Mansfield

...the heron, unseen for weeks, came flying
widewinged toward me, settled
just offshore on his post,
took up his vigil.
If you ask
why this cleared a fog from my spirit,
I have no answer.

Denise Levertov

Learn to be quiet enough to hear the
sound of the genuine within yourself,

so that you can hear it in other people.

Marian Wright Edelman

Why scurry about looking for the truth? It vibrates in every thing and every not-thing, right off the tip of your nose. Can you be still and see it in the mountain air? The pine tree? Yourself?

Hua Hu Ching

Ah, life grows lovely where you are.

Mathilde Blind

Beauty appears when something is completely and absolutely and openly itself.

Deena Metzger

To see her is to love her,
And love her but forever,
For Nature made her what she is,
And never made another.

Robert Burns

By having the courage to be herself, she put something wonderful in the world that was not there before.

Unknown

Some people are so beautiful. Not just in looks, not just in what they say, but in what they are.

Unknown

The kind of beauty I want most is the hard-to-get kind that comes from within—strength, courage, dignity.

Ruby Dee

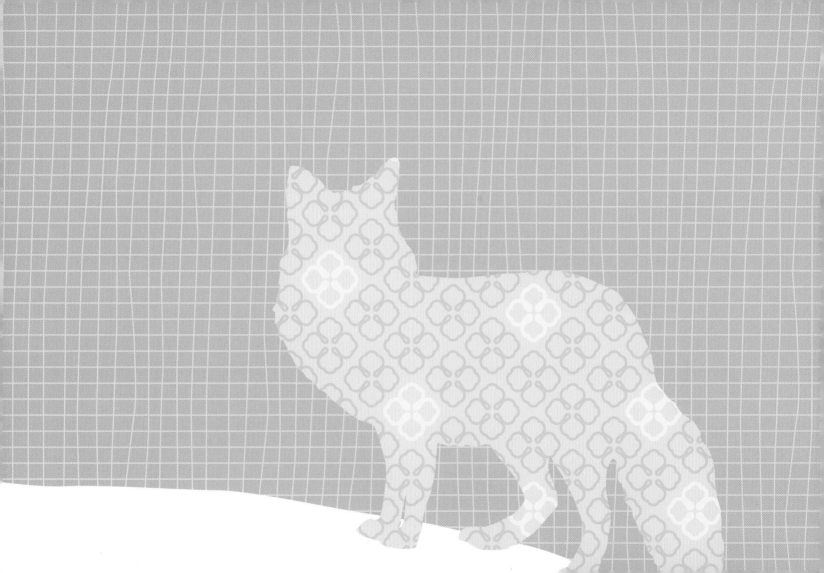

Strong is the soul, and wise, and beautiful.

Matthew Arnold

Deep in their roots all flowers keep the light.

Theodore Roethke

Like water, be gentle and strong.
Be gentle enough to follow the natural
paths of the earth, and strong enough to
rise up and reshape the world.

Elizabeth Berg

She has achieved success who has gained the love of her children; who has left the world better than she found it; who has never lacked appreciation of earth's beauty; who has looked for the best in others and given the best she had.

Mrs. A.J. Stanley

A single rose can be a garden...

...a single friend, a world.

Leo Buscaglia

Hold out your hands to feel the luxury of the sunbeams.

Helen Keller

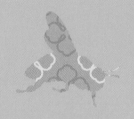

Some poems are never finished.

Jayne Cortez

Try to keep your soul young and quivering...
and to imagine right up to the brink of
death that life is only beginning.

George Sand

In July, when I bury my nose in a hazel bush, I feel fifteen years old again. It's good! It smells of love!

Camille Corot

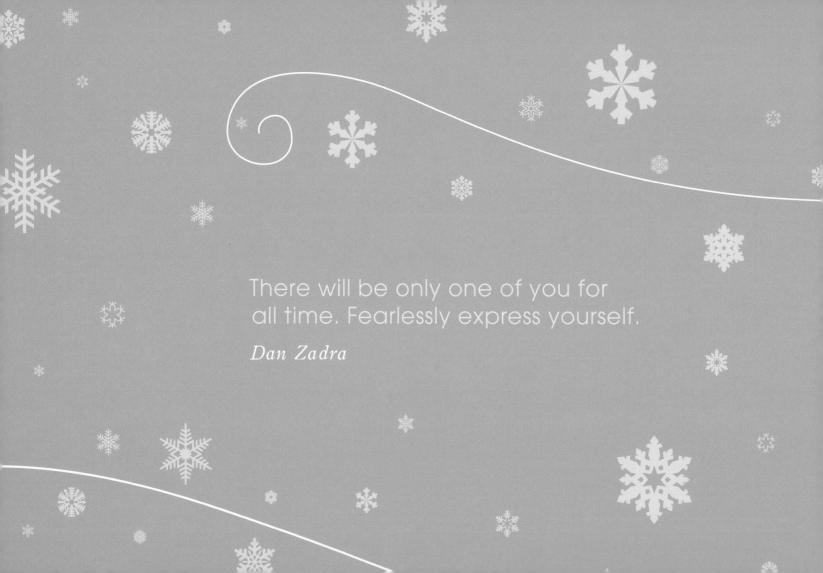

There will be only one of you for
all time. Fearlessly express yourself.

Dan Zadra

To sing is to love and affirm, to fly and soar, to coast into the hearts of the people who listen, to tell them that life is to live,

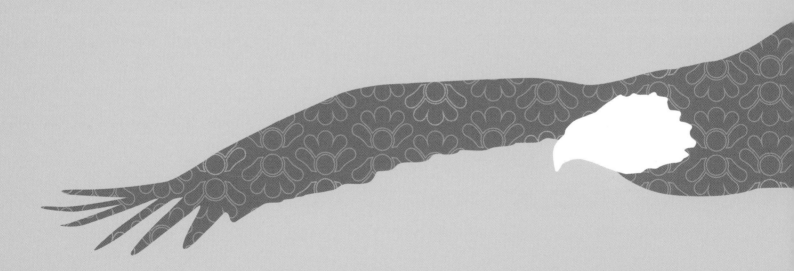

that life is theirs, that nothing is a promise,
but that beauty exists, and must be
hunted for and found....

Joan Baez

Forget not that the earth delights to feel your bare
feet, and the winds long to play with your hair.

Khalil Gibran

Treasure this day and treasure yourself.
Truly, neither will ever happen again.

Ray Bradbury